Uncle Sam

Terry Allan Hicks

mc **Marshall Cavendish**
Benchmark

Marshall Cavendish Benchmark
99 White Plains Road
Tarrytown, New York 10591-9001
www.marshallcavendish.us

Library of Congress Cataloging-in-Publication Data
Hicks, Terry Allan.
Uncle Sam / by Terry Allan Hicks.
p. cm. — (Symbols of America)
Summary: "An exporation of the origins and history of Uncle Sam and the real man, Samuel Wilson, who inspired this beloved symbol of America"—Provided by publisher.
  Includes bibliographical references (p. 38) and index.
  ISBN-13: 978-0-7614-2137-5
  ISBN-10: 0-7614-2137-8
1. Uncle Sam (Symbolic character)—Juvenile literature. 2. Wilson, Samuel, 1766–1854—Juvenile literature. 3. United States—Biography—Juvenile literature. I. Title. II. Series.

E179.H63 2006
398.2'0973'02—dc22
2005020616

Photo research by Anne Burns Images

Front cover: Corbis/Swim Ink 2 LLC
Back cover: U.S. Postal Service

The photographs in this book are used by permission and through the courtesy of: *Corbis:* Carl & Ann Purcell, 1; Bettman, 4, 8, 23, 24, 27; Philip Gould, 7; Poodles Rock, 12; Swim Ink 2 LLC, 28; Corbis, 31; George Contorakes, 35. *Rensselaer County Historical Society:* 11, 20. *North Wind Picture Archives:* 15, 16, 19. *U.S. Postal Service:* 32.

Series design by Adam Mietlowski

Printed in Malaysia

1 3 5 6 4 2

Contents

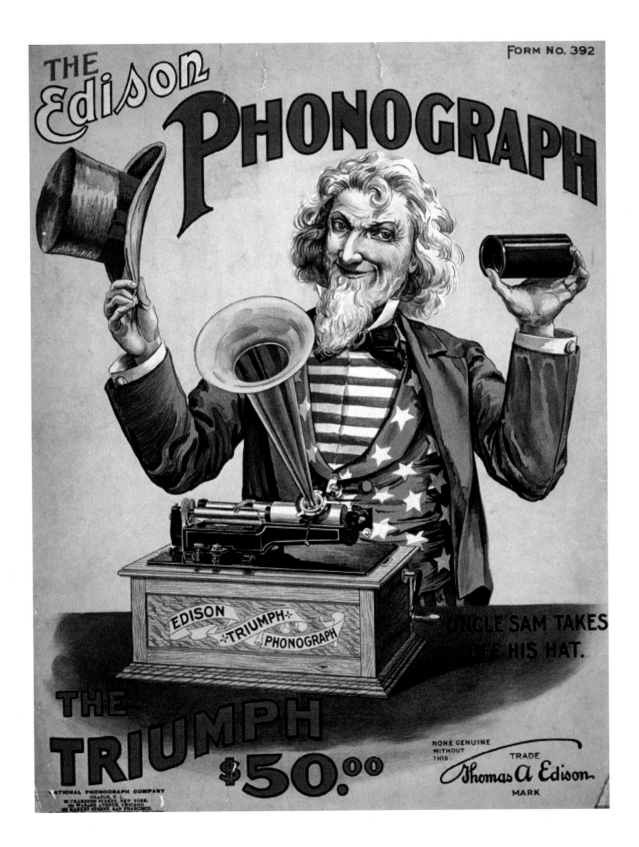

CHAPTER ONE

America's Favorite Uncle

Uncle Sam is one of America's best-known and best-loved symbols.

Every year, at Fourth of July parades across the country, millions of people proudly wave to their Uncle Sam as he marches by. But that is not the only place they can see him. Uncle Sam has appeared in thousands of paintings, *illustrations,* cartoons, and posters. He is quite a salesman, too. His image has been used to sell everything from airplanes to canned soup.

◀ *In this early advertisement, Uncle Sam displays an amazing new machine, the record player.*

Uncle Sam is nearly always shown with a white beard, wearing a tall stars-and-stripes top hat. His pants often have red and white stripes. A red bow tie, white shirt, and blue coat are also usually part of his all-American outfit.

What he looks like, though, isn't nearly as important as what he stands for. Uncle Sam *symbolizes* the way many Americans see themselves. He is friendly, cheerful, and reminds many of a kindly old grandfather. But when the times call for it—as in periods of war—his mood changes, and he appears grim and serious.

A tall Uncle Sam gives one of his fans a very high five. ▶

Uncle Sam is a *patriotic* symbol to people around the world. But few realize that the character of Uncle Sam was based on a real man.

His story begins in Troy, New York, in the spring of 1813. At the time, the United States was fighting a war with Great Britain, the country that ruled the thirteen colonies until the American Revolution. This *conflict* was called the War of 1812.

Troy, a town on the Hudson River, was an important gathering point for the soldiers about to invade the British colony of Canada. One day, as the story goes, a visitor saw barrels of meat for the Army being unloaded. The barrels were marked US—for United States. Not knowing what the *initials* stood for, the visitor asked a worker what they meant.

◀ *Many of the battles in the War of 1812 were fought on the water. Here, Oliver Perry, with his sword drawn, leads an attack against the British on Lake Erie.*

The worker replied, jokingly, that the barrels belonged to "Uncle Sam." But he was not talking about the red-white-and-blue symbol of the United States. Instead he meant his boss, Samuel Wilson, a local merchant, also known by the nickname Uncle Sam.

Soon the story was repeated in the houses and taverns of Troy. Before long, "Uncle Sam" became the phrase people there used to refer to the United States government. Soon it was even being used in print. On September 7, 1813, an *editorial* in a local newspaper, the *Troy Post*, referred to the United States government as Uncle Sam. Barely a month later, an editorial in Boston's *Columbian Sentinel* did the same. Uncle Sam was on his way to becoming a national figure.

In this mural, Samuel Wilson is shown along the docks of Troy. He worked hard for the war effort, packing and shipping barrels full of meat. ▶

CHAPTER TWO

The Real Uncle Sam

Samuel Wilson was born on September 13, 1766, in Menotomy (now Arlington), Massachusetts. He was one of thirteen children born to Edward and Lucy Wilson.

Young Samuel and his family may have witnessed one of the most famous events in American history. It is said that on the night of April 18, 1775—when Samuel was just eight years old—he and his family woke to the sound of a lone horseman riding past. It was Paul Revere, on his "midnight ride" to warn the patriots of Massachusetts that British soldiers were approaching from Boston.

This illustration of a scene from the American Revolution shows Paul Revere's famous ride to warn the colonists of a coming attack.

By the time the British reached the town of Lexington, less than 5 miles (8 kilometers) down the road, 70 *minutemen* were waiting. Young Samuel Wilson's father was among them. In the battle that followed, the first of the American Revolution, eight minutemen were killed, and the colonists were forced to retreat. Later that day, in another battle in nearby Concord, it was the British who were defeated.

The battle of Lexington began the Revolutionary War.

SLAUGHTERING & PACKING.

THE undersigned having two large and convenient SLAUGHTER-HOUSES, beg leave to acquaint their customers, and others, that they will be enabled to *kill, cut* and *pack* 150 head of Cattle per day; and, from their local situation, pledge themselves to accommodate those who may favour them with a call, on terms as low as can be obtained in the State.

They have on hand a large supply of BARRELS and SALT, which will be disposed of on the lowest terms,

All those who shall be under the necessity of waiting 24 hours for their cattle to be slaughtered, shall have them pastured free of expence.   E. & S. Wilson.

Troy, Sept. 24, 1805.   56

Later, Samuel Wilson also enlisted in the Army, though he was just fourteen or fifteen years old. After the war, he returned to his family, who had moved to Mason, New Hampshire.

In 1789 Sam and his older brother Ebenezer left New Hampshire in search of work. They walked all the way from Mason to Troy, New York—a distance of almost 175 miles (280 kilometers). Settling in Troy, the brothers learned the brick-making trade. Eventually they built their own brick factory. In 1793 they started a *meatpacking* business, called the E. & S. Wilson company. They later built a meatpacking plant and dock on the Hudson River. That way, they could ship meat down the river to New York City.

Ships unloading cargo at the New York City docks in the 1800s. Some of the goods made their way up the Hudson River to Troy.
Inset: An advertisement from the Troy Gazette spreads the word about the Wilson brother's meatpacking company.

In 1797 Sam returned to New Hampshire to marry Betsey Mann. (One of Betsey's cousins was John Chapman, who became famous as Johnny Appleseed. He spent most of his life wandering in the wilderness, planting apple orchards.) The couple settled in Troy. They were known to almost everyone in the area as Uncle Sam and Aunt Betsey. They eventually had four children.

Johnny Appleseed is known for the many orchards he planted on the frontier. ▶

When the War of 1812 started, E. & S. Wilson began supplying beef and pork to the Army. It was at this time that barrels stamped US first appeared on the docks of Troy. It would be a while, however, before the face and name of Uncle Sam—the well-known character—would be adopted as a symbol of the nation.

◀ *The Hudson River port of Troy, New York, shown in 1825.*

CHAPTER THREE

A New Symbol of America

Uncle Sam was a widely used name as early as 1813. But it was not until 1830 that the popular character was given a face. That year, a drawing in a newspaper appeared. It illustrated an editorial *criticizing* President Andrew Jackson. It showed Uncle Sam as a chubby, sad-looking fellow. In a sign of things to come, he was wearing clothes made from the American flag.

At first, Uncle Sam was drawn a number of different ways. An early political cartoon shows him eyeing a prize: the island of Cuba. ▶

In the years that followed, more artists drew Uncle Sam. An illustration from 1854—the year Samuel Wilson died—shows Uncle Sam with no stripes wearing only a plain top hat and tail-coat. Over the next few years, artists showed Uncle Sam in many different ways: fat, thin, old, young, and dressed in a variety of clothes. Few of the pictures they made looked anything like the real Sam Wilson, who was muscular and never wore a beard.

◀ *Uncle Sam forgets about politics long enough to enjoy a baseball game. Through the years, his image kept popping up in more and more places.*

Because photography was expensive in the 1800s, newspapers and magazines used artists' drawings and cartoons instead. One artist, more than any other, gave Uncle Sam the look we know today. His name was Thomas Nast. He drew political cartoons for the popular magazine *Harper's Weekly*. For many years, beginning in the 1870s, Nast drew Uncle Sam as a thin older man dressed like the American flag.

Thomas Nast was one of America's most important cartoonists.

I WANT YOU
FOR U.S. ARMY
NEAREST RECRUITING STATION

Uncle Sam had the same look in James Montgomery Flagg's cover illustration for the July 6, 1916, issue of *Leslie's Weekly* magazine. In it, a stern Uncle Sam points straight out and asks the readers what they are doing to get ready for World War One. The United States would enter the war the following year.

This is the image that James Montgomery Flagg drew for Leslie's Weekly. *The United States Army would use the illustration on one of its well-known posters.*

The United States government asked Flagg to turn his illustration into a *recruiting* poster for the Army. With its headline changed to the now famous phrase "I Want You," it *inspired* thousands of young Americans to fight for their country. It was *reproduced* more than four million times in 1917–1918 alone. The poster was used again during World War Two, at the request of President Franklin D. Roosevelt. As recently as the year 2000, the United States military was still using Flagg's illustration.

James Montgomery Flagg with the famous Uncle Sam recruiting poster that he created.

▶

Unlike some other symbols of America, Uncle Sam has never lost his appeal. He still appears in hundreds of cartoons and advertisements every year. And, of course, he still greets Americans at Fourth of July parades and events across the country.

In 1961, Congress passed a *resolution* honoring Samuel Wilson as the real man behind the character of Uncle Sam. Then in 1998—at the request of the people of Troy—the United States Postal Service honored him with an official stamp.

◀ *The United States government honored the spirit of Uncle Sam by issuing a special postage stamp that bears his image.*

Today, after nearly two hundred years, Uncle Sam is still a very busy fellow. He reminds Americans of their proud past, and especially of the many wars that have shaped the nation's history. Most of all, he helps recruit soldiers, asking Americans to serve the country they call home.

Hats off to you, Uncle Sam! ▶

Glossary

conflict—A war or disagreement.

criticize—To find fault with someone or something.

editorial—A newspaper article that expresses an opinion.

illustration—A drawing or artwork.

initials—The first letters of each word in a phrase or name, as in U.S. meaning "United States."

inspire—To excite or move someone to action.

meatpacking—Preparing and packaging meat for people to eat.

minuteman—A colonist who was ready to fight the British "at a minute's notice."

patriotic—Showing the love and support of one's country.

recruit—To encourage people to join an organization, such as the Army.

reproduce—To make copies.

resolution—A course of action a group of people has decided to follow.

symbolize—To represent or stand for a group, nation, or idea.

Find Out More

Books

Bateman, Teresa. *Red, White, Blue, and Uncle Who?* New York: Holiday House, 2001.

Holub, Joan. *Who Was Johnny Appleseed?* New York: Grosset & Dunlap, 2005.

Marcovitz, Hal. *Uncle Sam.* Philadelphia: Mason Crest, 2003.

Raatma, Lucy. *Paul Revere's Ride.* Minneapolis: Compass Point, 2003.

West, Delno C., and Jean M. West. *Uncle Sam and Old Glory: Symbols of America.* New York: Atheneum Books for Young Readers, 2000.

Web Sites

Activity: Frozen Uncle Sams

http://familyfun.go.com/recipes/kids/feature/famf0600icecream/
famf0600icecream4.html

American Treasures of the Library of Congress: "The Most Famous Poster"
http://www.loc.gov/exhibits/treasures/trm015.html

Congress for Kids: An Uncle Sam–Guided Tour
http://congressforkids.net/cartoonintro.htm

Uncle Sam's Grave
http://home. nycap.rr.com/contents/us_grave.html

"Uncle Sam's World in Political Cartoons" by Jim Zwick
http://www.boondocksnet.com/gallery/us_intro.html

Index